PERMISSION SLIPS...

FOR YOUR HEART & SOUL

PATRICIA J. MOSCA

ISBN-13: 9781937137861

Copyright © 2012 by Patricia J. Mosca

This book is a work of fiction. Names, characters, places, and incidents either are products of the author's imagination or are used fictitiously. Any resemblance to actual events or locales or persons, living or dead, is entirely coincidental.

All rights reserved. No part of this book may be reproduced or transmitted in any form or by any means, electronic or mechanical, including photocopying, recording, or by any information storage and retrieval system, without permission in writing from the Publisher.

StoryPeople Press
P.O. Box 7
Decorah, IA 52101
USA
563.382.8060
563.382.0263 FAX
800.476.7178

storypeople@storypeople.com
www.storypeople.com
storypeoplepress.com

Library of Congress Control Number: 2011944076

First Edition: April, 2012

Introduction

There was a point in my life where I was in transition. I was stuck and I didn't know where to go, what to do or even where to begin. In a conversation with a friend, she asked me what would help me get unstuck. It was in that moment that I realized PERMISSION would help me! Permission is important to all of us because it often is what we need the most and we do not allow ourselves to have it.

Here are 52 permission slips that I came up with, and I hope they help you when you need them. Cut them out if you want to and tape them on the mirror, on the fridge, on your wall, or in your car. You have permission to use them as often and as many times as you need to...

With all my heart I thank my good husband, Michael, who was my biggest fan, for supporting me and giving me permission to be myself! Michael passed three weeks before I received word that this book was to be published, but I know he would be very proud, as he always believed in me even when I had my doubts. My children, Lea and Jason, who have brought me more joy than I can ever express, And to my littlest love, Collin, who shows me how to have permission every day to live life to the fullest! To my family and friends who have always cheered me on my deepest gratitude. A big round of applause goes out to StoryPeople Press for all the color and joy they have brought into my life and for giving me permission not to be afraid!

Artfully Yours,

Patricia J. Mosca

PERMISSION SLIPS...

FOR YOUR HEART & SOUL

StoryPeople Press

To all those in need of permission,
from my heart to yours.

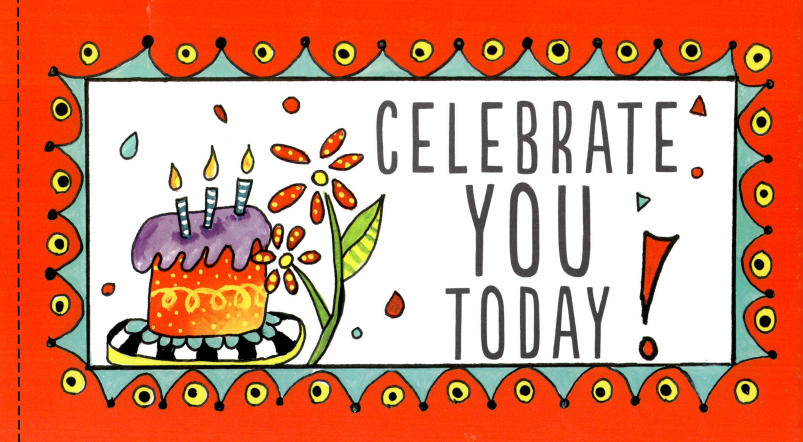

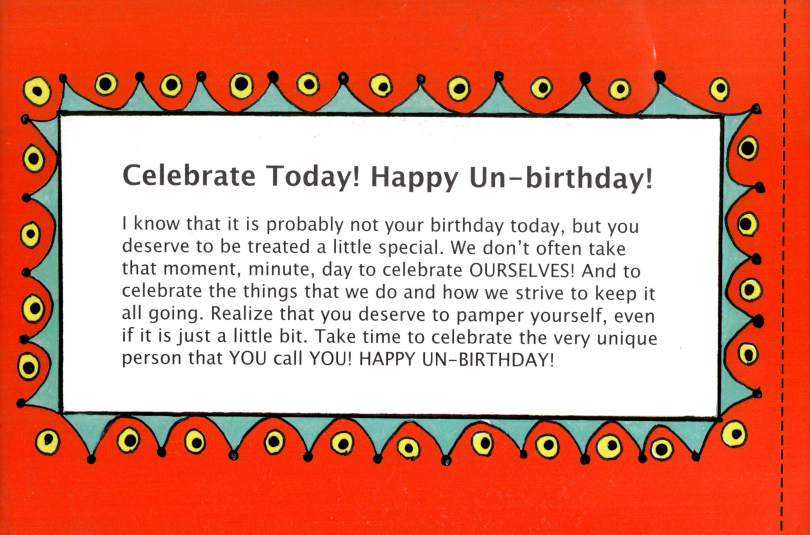

Celebrate Today! Happy Un-birthday!

I know that it is probably not your birthday today, but you deserve to be treated a little special. We don't often take that moment, minute, day to celebrate OURSELVES! And to celebrate the things that we do and how we strive to keep it all going. Realize that you deserve to pamper yourself, even if it is just a little bit. Take time to celebrate the very unique person that YOU call YOU! HAPPY UN-BIRTHDAY!

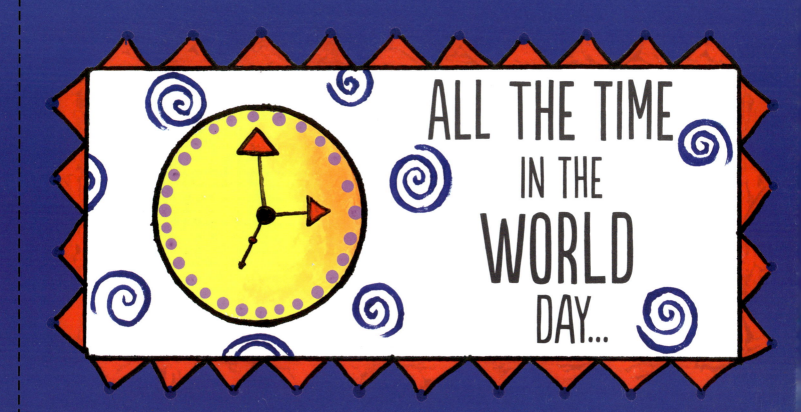

There is no deadline. Today you have all the time in the world to do whatever you want.

Sometimes we are so wrapped up in life, and projects with deadlines, that we are in great need of all the time in the world. Just to do whatever tasks you want to do for no other reason than because YOU WANT TO DO THEM! Whip out this permission slip and let yourself have a ball! Take a day and put some of your dreams into motion for yourself. After all, you have the time.

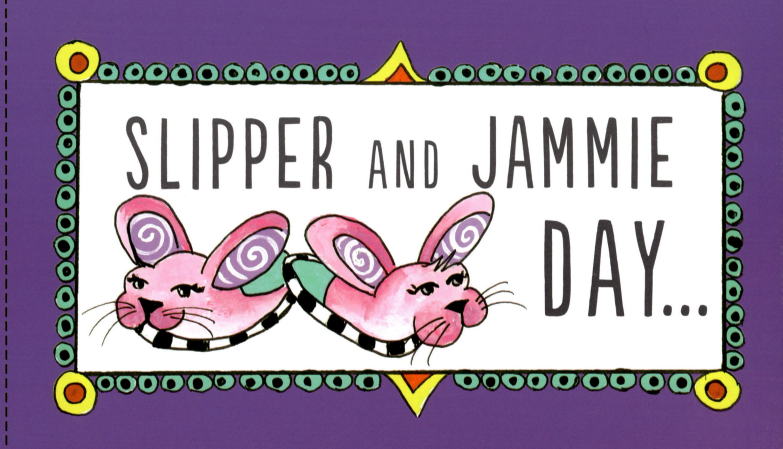

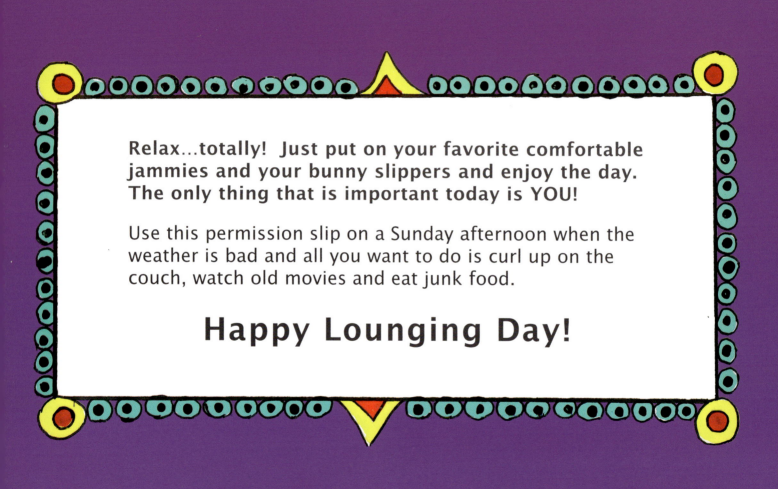

Relax...totally! Just put on your favorite comfortable jammies and your bunny slippers and enjoy the day. The only thing that is important today is YOU!

Use this permission slip on a Sunday afternoon when the weather is bad and all you want to do is curl up on the couch, watch old movies and eat junk food.

Happy Lounging Day!

Permission to RECHARGE! Try to escape and use 30 minutes today for yourself. This recharge time will keep your mind sharp and your energy level higher.

That's right...give yourself permission to escape from your everyday routine for a moment or two just to be by yourself. If you work in an office, take that lunchtime to take a walk, listen to music on your iPod, run, exercise or just go to a nearby park and listen to the birds sing. If you have a family, slip out of the room and find a quiet spot of your own. You will feel more connected to who you are and what you can accomplish. There is nothing selfish about wanting a little RECHARGE TIME. Plug yourself into YOU!

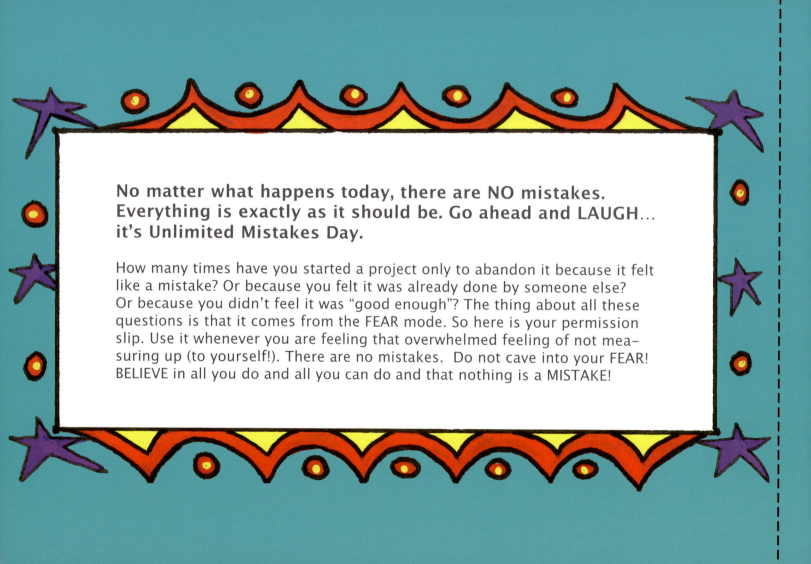

No matter what happens today, there are NO mistakes. Everything is exactly as it should be. Go ahead and LAUGH… it's Unlimited Mistakes Day.

How many times have you started a project only to abandon it because it felt like a mistake? Or because you felt it was already done by someone else? Or because you didn't feel it was "good enough"? The thing about all these questions is that it comes from the FEAR mode. So here is your permission slip. Use it whenever you are feeling that overwhelmed feeling of not measuring up (to yourself!). There are no mistakes. Do not cave into your FEAR! BELIEVE in all you do and all you can do and that nothing is a MISTAKE!

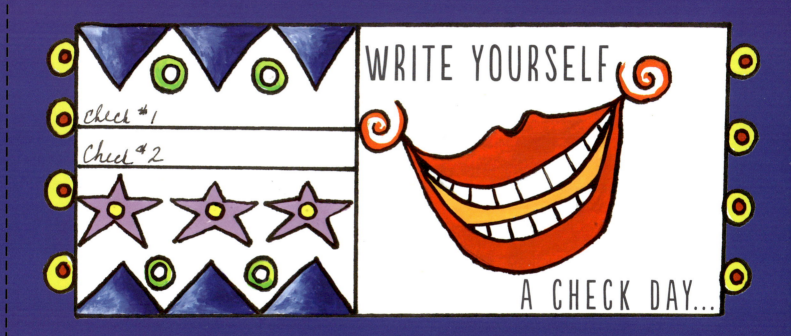

This slip gives you permission to write yourself a personal blank check, a happiness check, a laughter check, a dream check, checking in with yourself, or a dream-your-own-dream-without-guilt check. Go ahead... fill in the blanks.

So many days go by when we give permission to everyone BUT ourselves! Today is the day that you can write a blank check to yourself for anything YOU need. You don't have to wait for anyone to give you this permission slip. You have one right here!

Shine…glow…bask in your sunshine. You deserve it. It is your truth. So let it shine, let it shine, let it shine!

Were you told when you were young "NOT TO BRAG"? Today you have permission to SHINE! This slip allows you to honor yourself and your accomplishments. It is not bragging but rather speaking your truth. Once you begin to do this for yourself, you will find that the feeling that you get from that honor makes you just want to get up and achieve MORE! So go ahead… LET YOURSELF SHINE TODAY!

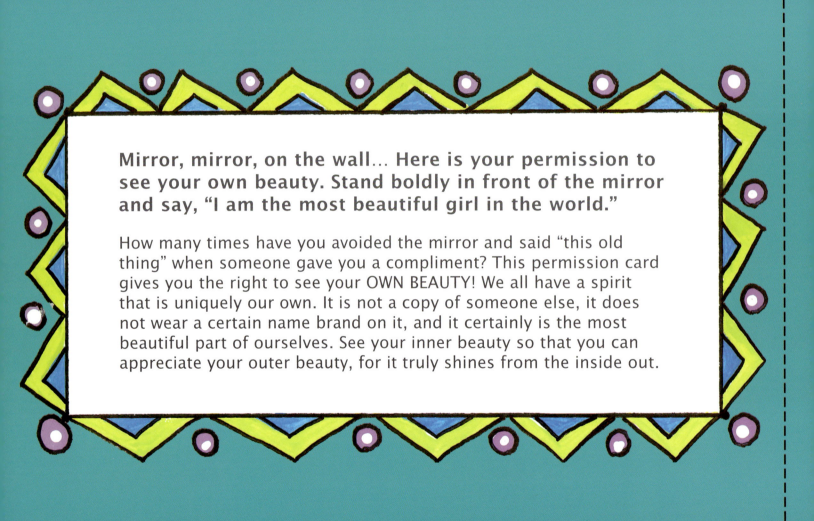

Mirror, mirror, on the wall... Here is your permission to see your own beauty. Stand boldly in front of the mirror and say, "I am the most beautiful girl in the world."

How many times have you avoided the mirror and said "this old thing" when someone gave you a compliment? This permission card gives you the right to see your OWN BEAUTY! We all have a spirit that is uniquely our own. It is not a copy of someone else, it does not wear a certain name brand on it, and it certainly is the most beautiful part of ourselves. See your inner beauty so that you can appreciate your outer beauty, for it truly shines from the inside out.

How many times have you missed an opportunity to say something that you wish you had said? Here is a permission slip to do just that...to not miss the opportunities that are placed in front of you.

As if by some magic, people seem to know exactly what we are thinking or exactly what we want without us having to say a single word. We often wait till it is too late to say the things we want and need to say. This permission card says you can say all the wonderful, or even some of the non-wonderful, things that you need to say without anger or without regret. When we speak our truths from our heart, people tend to listen and hear us. So go ahead...it is a precious gift that you give yourself to be heard!

Well, we all know that eBay has "it" and now so do you! This gives you the permission to do "it," whatever "it" may be.

There are quite a few things that we label as "IT." eBay has "IT," Nike has "IT," we do "IT," we want "IT" and often times we can't have "IT"! But this is your permission slip to go ahead and do whatever "IT" is. Whatever "IT" is that you are dreaming of, you can go out and capture. Sometimes we use "IT" as an excuse, but today you can GO FOR IT!

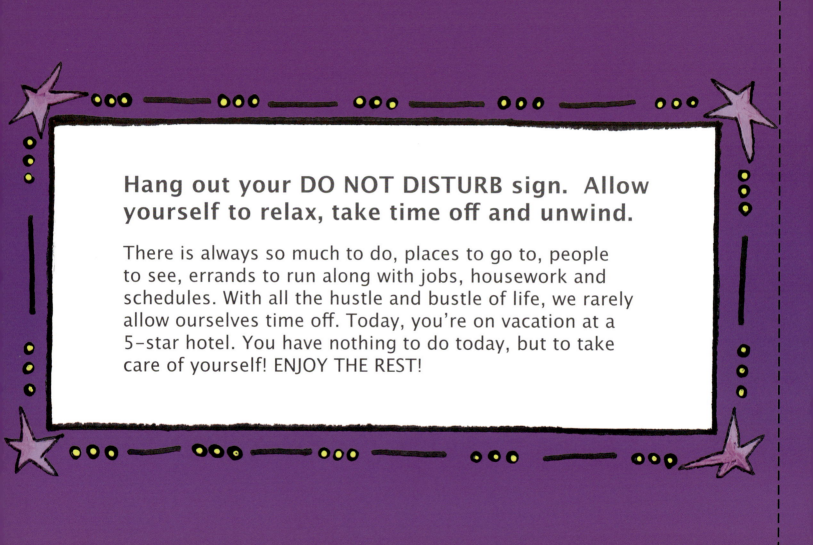

Hang out your DO NOT DISTURB sign. Allow yourself to relax, take time off and unwind.

There is always so much to do, places to go to, people to see, errands to run along with jobs, housework and schedules. With all the hustle and bustle of life, we rarely allow ourselves time off. Today, you're on vacation at a 5-star hotel. You have nothing to do today, but to take care of yourself! ENJOY THE REST!

Do you keep telling yourself that you're going to change something, or break some habit? All you have to do is start with a thought, start with a moment, a minute…WOW! It just may not be as hard as you think.

So many times we all say we are going to do something, and then for whatever reason it gets passed over. Then we fumble around and look for answers. Well, today you have permission to go back and start that something. Start with just thinking of it, then thinking how you are going to go about it, and then jump in and start. No time like the present!

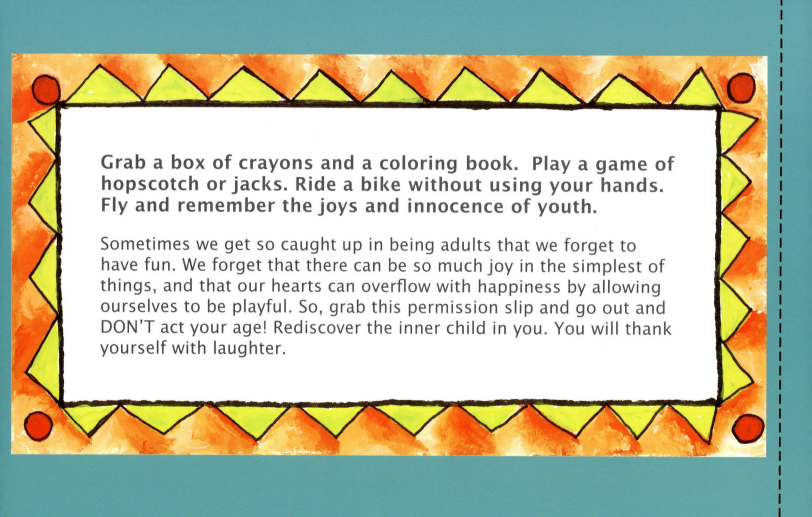

Grab a box of crayons and a coloring book. Play a game of hopscotch or jacks. Ride a bike without using your hands. Fly and remember the joys and innocence of youth.

Sometimes we get so caught up in being adults that we forget to have fun. We forget that there can be so much joy in the simplest of things, and that our hearts can overflow with happiness by allowing ourselves to be playful. So, grab this permission slip and go out and DON'T act your age! Rediscover the inner child in you. You will thank yourself with laughter.

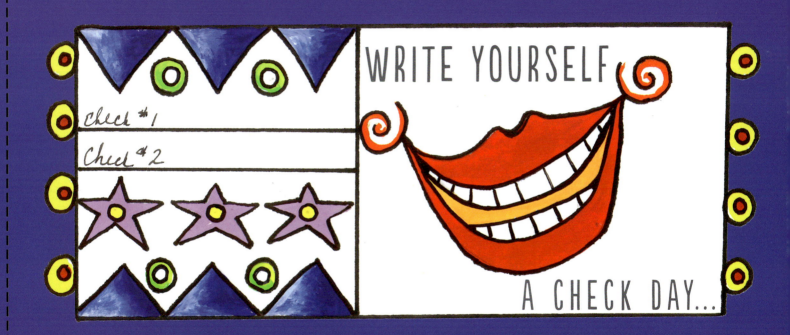

This slip gives you permission to write yourself a personal blank check, a happiness check, a laughter check, a dream check, checking in with yourself, or a dream-your-own-dream-without-guilt check. Go ahead... fill in the blanks.

So many days go by when we give permission to everyone BUT ourselves! Today is the day that you can write a blank check to yourself for anything YOU need. You don't have to wait for anyone to give you this permission slip. You have one right here!

Shine…glow…bask in your sunshine. You deserve it. It is your truth. So let it shine, let it shine, let it shine!

Were you told when you were young "NOT TO BRAG"? Today you have permission to SHINE! This slip allows you to honor yourself and your accomplishments. It is not bragging but rather speaking your truth. Once you begin to do this for yourself, you will find that the feeling that you get from that honor makes you just want to get up and achieve MORE! So go ahead… LET YOURSELF SHINE TODAY!

Mirror, mirror, on the wall… Here is your permission to see your own beauty. Stand boldly in front of the mirror and say, "I am the most beautiful girl in the world."

How many times have you avoided the mirror and said "this old thing" when someone gave you a compliment? This permission card gives you the right to see your OWN BEAUTY! We all have a spirit that is uniquely our own. It is not a copy of someone else, it does not wear a certain name brand on it, and it certainly is the most beautiful part of ourselves. See your inner beauty so that you can appreciate your outer beauty, for it truly shines from the inside out.

How many times have you missed an opportunity to say something that you wish you had said? Here is a permission slip to do just that...to not miss the opportunities that are placed in front of you.

As if by some magic, people seem to know exactly what we are thinking or exactly what we want without us having to say a single word. We often wait till it is too late to say the things we want and need to say. This permission card says you can say all the wonderful, or even some of the non-wonderful, things that you need to say without anger or without regret. When we speak our truths from our heart, people tend to listen and hear us. So go ahead...it is a precious gift that you give yourself to be heard!

Well, we all know that eBay has "it" and now so do you! This gives you the permission to do "it," whatever "it" may be.

There are quite a few things that we label as "IT." eBay has "IT," Nike has "IT," we do "IT," we want "IT" and often times we can't have "IT"! But this is your permission slip to go ahead and do whatever "IT" is. Whatever "IT" is that you are dreaming of, you can go out and capture. Sometimes we use "IT" as an excuse, but today you can GO FOR IT!

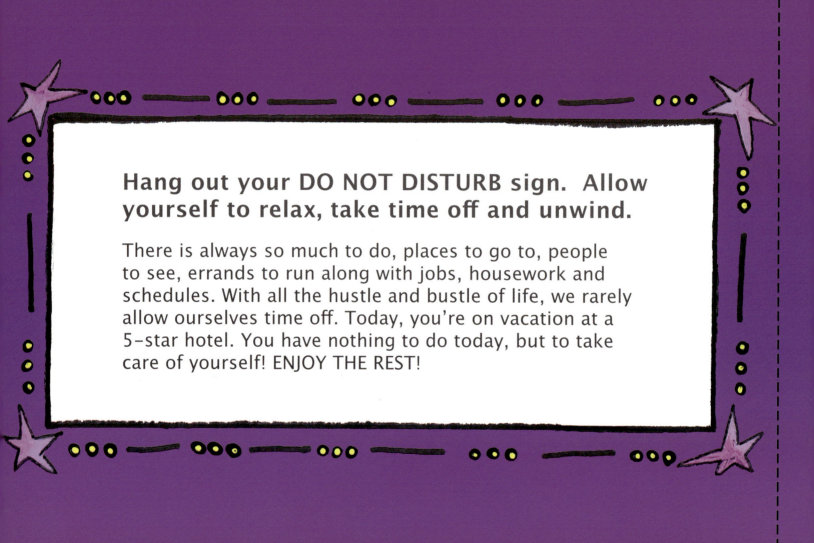

Hang out your DO NOT DISTURB sign. Allow yourself to relax, take time off and unwind.

There is always so much to do, places to go to, people to see, errands to run along with jobs, housework and schedules. With all the hustle and bustle of life, we rarely allow ourselves time off. Today, you're on vacation at a 5-star hotel. You have nothing to do today, but to take care of yourself! ENJOY THE REST!

Do you keep telling yourself that you're going to change something, or break some habit? All you have to do is start with a thought, start with a moment, a minute…WOW! It just may not be as hard as you think.

So many times we all say we are going to do something, and then for whatever reason it gets passed over. Then we fumble around and look for answers. Well, today you have permission to go back and start that something. Start with just thinking of it, then thinking how you are going to go about it, and then jump in and start. No time like the present!

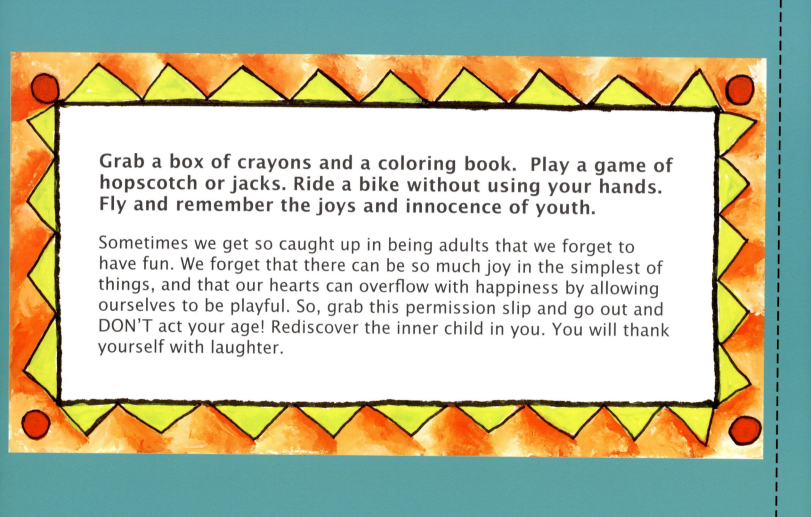

Grab a box of crayons and a coloring book. Play a game of hopscotch or jacks. Ride a bike without using your hands. Fly and remember the joys and innocence of youth.

Sometimes we get so caught up in being adults that we forget to have fun. We forget that there can be so much joy in the simplest of things, and that our hearts can overflow with happiness by allowing ourselves to be playful. So, grab this permission slip and go out and DON'T act your age! Rediscover the inner child in you. You will thank yourself with laughter.

Listen to the messages your heart offers you. Hear the gratitude for all that surrounds you. Reawaken to your passions, your feelings and your love.

You can do this simply by making a list of five things that you are grateful for today. Start with small things: a warm cup of coffee, the song of a bird outside your window, the smell of fresh mowed grass. Just know that once you start this practice, you will be releasing the messages that your heart has for you. You will find that you have so much to be grateful for. Reawaken yourself by releasing your heart's whispers.

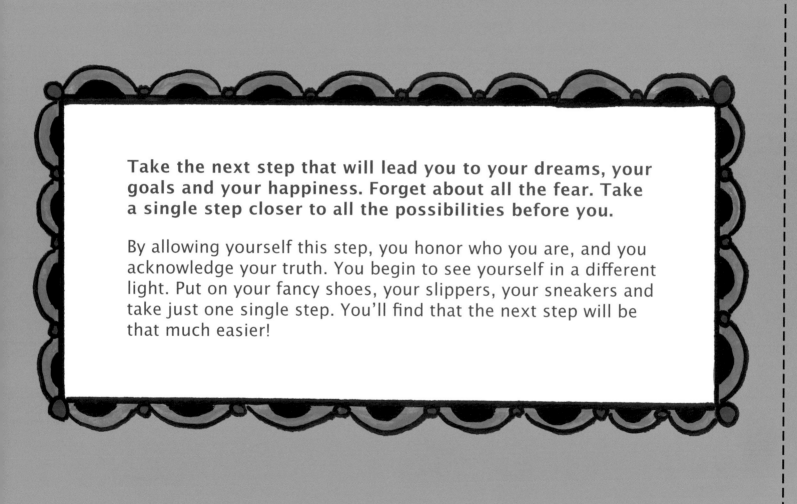

Take the next step that will lead you to your dreams, your goals and your happiness. Forget about all the fear. Take a single step closer to all the possibilities before you.

By allowing yourself this step, you honor who you are, and you acknowledge your truth. You begin to see yourself in a different light. Put on your fancy shoes, your slippers, your sneakers and take just one single step. You'll find that the next step will be that much easier!

Recognize your courage today. Go beyond your own limits. Use your shield and break down your own walls. Feel your victory joy.

Fear is something that overcomes all of us on any given day! But what if you just stepped back and looked at what is causing that fear, and realize that you are so much bigger than anything you could possibly be afraid of. You can carry your own shield and protect yourself from fear by uttering the word COURAGE as your battle cry. Remember, if you did not have fear, you would not have anything to conquer.

What is NO day? It is the day you can actually say NO to things people ask of you and you really do not want to do. Anyone who values and respects you will understand. Affirm your own needs and views.

Here is permission to say NO to whatever it is that you really DO NOT WANT TO DO! No excuses, no guilt, no little white lies. People will be shocked at first, especially if you are a YES person. But, if they really value you, they will respect that you are being TRUE to yourself. The first NO is the hardest; it really does start to get better after that. Learn that you honor yourself and who you are! You just might be shocked at the positive reaction you get.

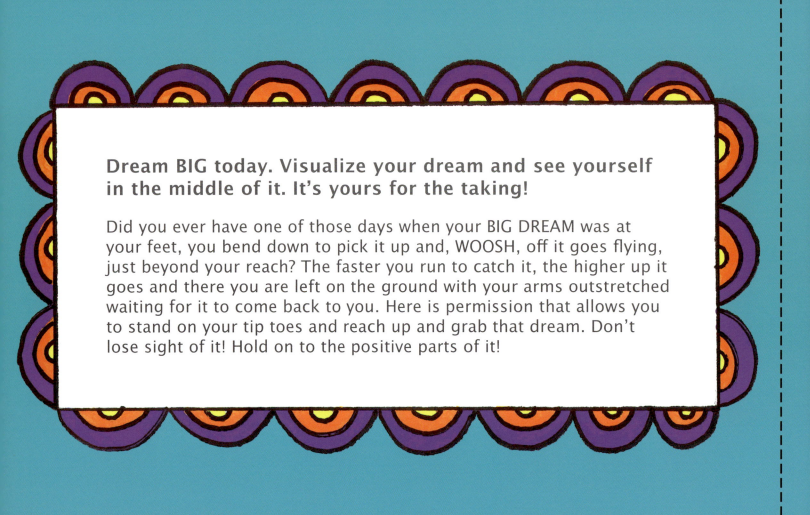

Dream BIG today. Visualize your dream and see yourself in the middle of it. It's yours for the taking!

Did you ever have one of those days when your BIG DREAM was at your feet, you bend down to pick it up and, WOOSH, off it goes flying, just beyond your reach? The faster you run to catch it, the higher up it goes and there you are left on the ground with your arms outstretched waiting for it to come back to you. Here is permission that allows you to stand on your tip toes and reach up and grab that dream. Don't lose sight of it! Hold on to the positive parts of it!

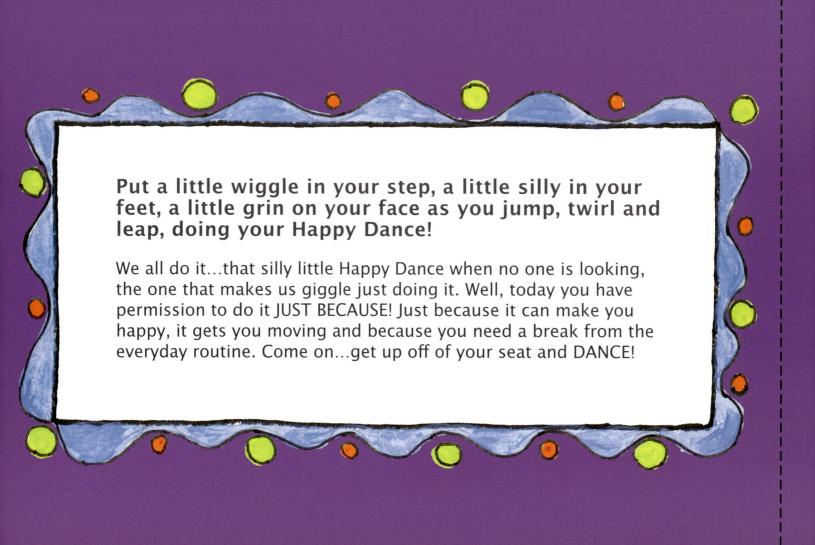

Put a little wiggle in your step, a little silly in your feet, a little grin on your face as you jump, twirl and leap, doing your Happy Dance!

We all do it…that silly little Happy Dance when no one is looking, the one that makes us giggle just doing it. Well, today you have permission to do it JUST BECAUSE! Just because it can make you happy, it gets you moving and because you need a break from the everyday routine. Come on…get up off of your seat and DANCE!

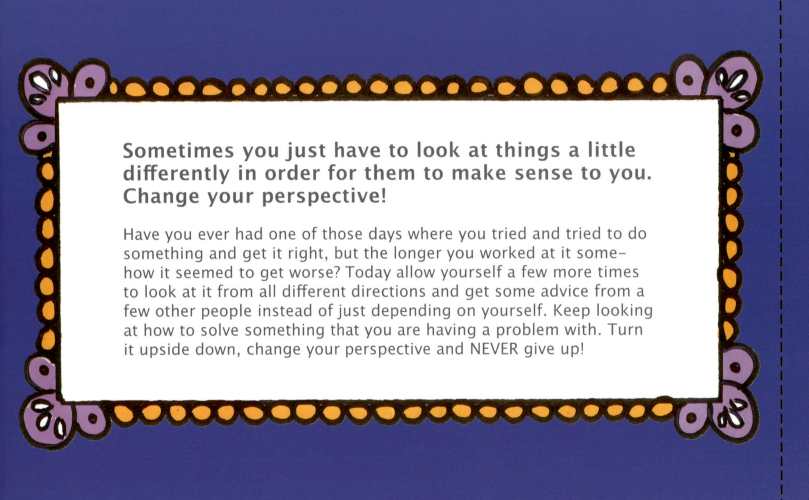

Sometimes you just have to look at things a little differently in order for them to make sense to you. Change your perspective!

Have you ever had one of those days where you tried and tried to do something and get it right, but the longer you worked at it somehow it seemed to get worse? Today allow yourself a few more times to look at it from all different directions and get some advice from a few other people instead of just depending on yourself. Keep looking at how to solve something that you are having a problem with. Turn it upside down, change your perspective and NEVER give up!

Stretch your boundaries. Reawaken your passions. Stretch your truth. You can do anything you want!

STRETCH! Let your mind wander over your moments and know that you can do anything you want.
STRETCH! So that you can open up some free time for yourself.
STRETCH! So that you can dream a little bit bigger.
STRETCH! So that you realize and honor your truths.
STRETCH! So that you believe and see the miracles before you.

Here is permission to start over, take another turn and roll the dice again. It may turn out just the way you dreamt it.

This is the permission slip to pick that unfinished item up and start it again. Or rework the project that did not look or feel right. Or just plain start over from scratch. You now can bypass the beating up stage and take another turn with a grin and a giggle. The best part about this card is YOU CAN USE IT OVER AND OVER AND OVER again! So go ahead, dig out those projects and roll the dice again.

Everyone has the "right" to be angry. But, by forgiving, you free up your peaceful energy to remain compassionate toward yourself and others. Even if it seems impossible, TRY to find the strength in your heart to forgive. It is so worth it!

We could be angry at ourselves, angry at a friend, or angry at a loved one. The person that the anger is directed at really does not matter. It is the energy of the anger that gets in our way. Negative energy brings MORE negative energy your way. By looking into our heart and really seeing that we want to live a full and wonderful life, we are able to search and find the tender spot of compassion. Today BREATHE a little deeper.

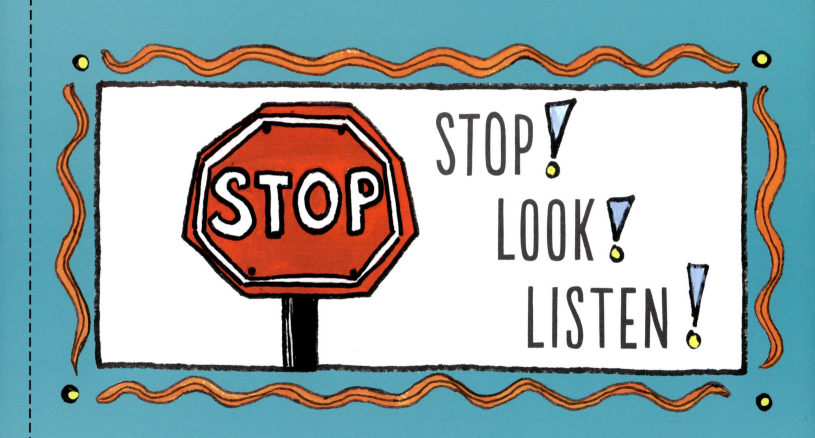

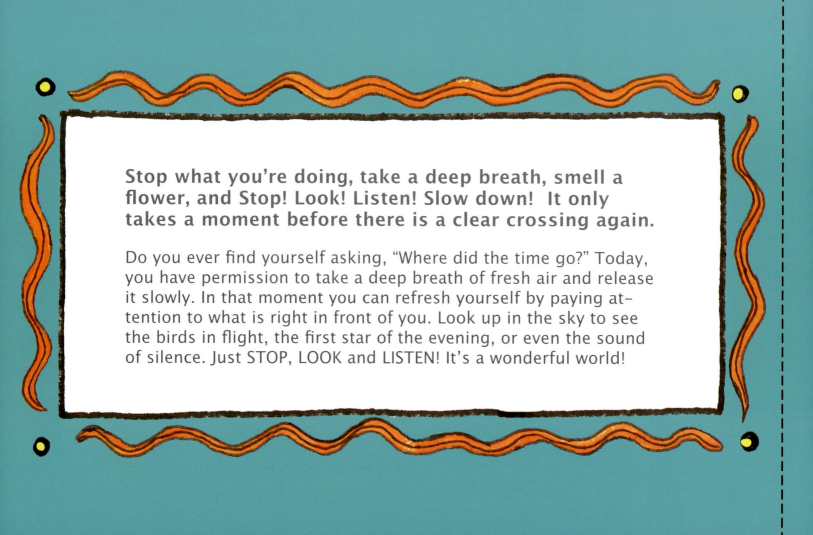

Stop what you're doing, take a deep breath, smell a flower, and Stop! Look! Listen! Slow down! It only takes a moment before there is a clear crossing again.

Do you ever find yourself asking, "Where did the time go?" Today, you have permission to take a deep breath of fresh air and release it slowly. In that moment you can refresh yourself by paying attention to what is right in front of you. Look up in the sky to see the birds in flight, the first star of the evening, or even the sound of silence. Just STOP, LOOK and LISTEN! It's a wonderful world!

Take five minutes to just stop all the noise today. Take a deep breath of PEACE and QUIET! Go ahead… indulge yourself.

Have you ever had one of those days where you thought, "If one more person says anything to me, I think I will just scream!"? Here is permission that allows you to take some time for yourself when that feeling starts to take you over. It doesn't really matter if it is five minutes or five hours, as long as you get to clear your head a little. Breathe deeply and you'll feel a bit more refreshed and ready to listen to that "one more person" with a smile on your face.

For whatever reason we often feel as if we do not deserve to be successful... BUT WE DO! The more you are aware of your successes, the more you become a magnet for it.

Why is it that when you have a moment of success you often make excuses for it, or you do not share it, for fear of feeling as if you are bragging? We all deserve success in whatever it is that we are doing whether it be personal success or professional success. No matter what your success is, you have to be aware of it, you have to honor it, and you have to make it yours. Make yourself a magnet for success... just by using this permission slip whenever needed.

If you need it, ask for help. There are people who love you and would be more than happy to lend a hand. It is not a sign of weakness.

Asking for help can bring us closer to where we want to be. It takes more courage to ask for help when you need it than to not ask for it. So go ahead, take off that "SUPER" cape that you tend to want to wear and reach out to someone if you need help. And if you know someone who needs your help, well… reach out to them! It will make you feel good because it's a WIN, WIN situation.

How many times have you thought about trying something new, but because you thought you had to be "perfect" at it, you pushed the thought away? Today, you can start putting that thought into motion.

So you have seen something in a magazine, or online, or in a book that you wanted to try to do, or perhaps there is a class that you want to take, but something is STOPPING you right in your tracks. Could it be? PERFECTION! Many of us do not want to look silly or look like we don't know what we are doing. So we lose out. Well…here you go! Permission to do something badly, (or at least what you consider badly). Just having the desire to do something new is good! So what do you want to try?

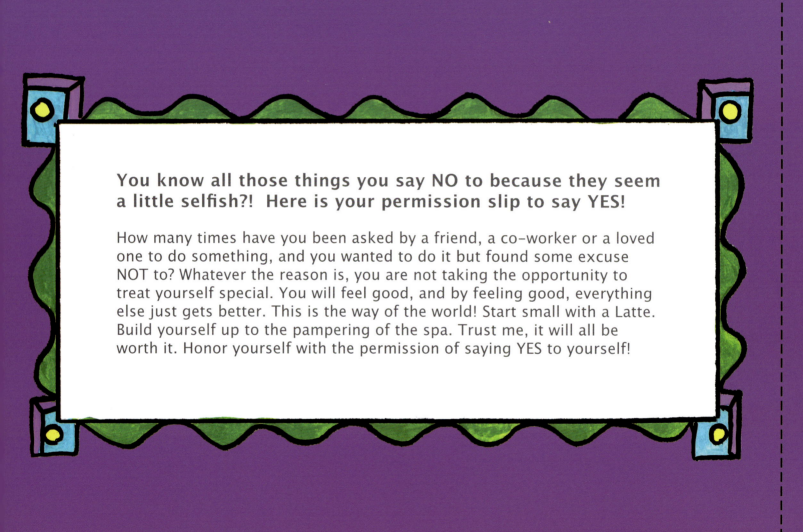

You know all those things you say NO to because they seem a little selfish?! Here is your permission slip to say YES!

How many times have you been asked by a friend, a co-worker or a loved one to do something, and you wanted to do it but found some excuse NOT to? Whatever the reason is, you are not taking the opportunity to treat yourself special. You will feel good, and by feeling good, everything else just gets better. This is the way of the world! Start small with a Latte. Build yourself up to the pampering of the spa. Trust me, it will all be worth it. Honor yourself with the permission of saying YES to yourself!

Let everything you do today be a "piece of cake." If it starts to become hard or frustrating, find the frosting and lick your fingers.

Why is it that we make things harder than they need to be sometimes? You look at a project and think, "Oh, I can't do that, it is going to be too hard!" So you don't even attempt to do it; then you get mad because you didn't do it. So, today, make it a piece of cake day. No matter what project or chore you have to do, just take a finger full of frosting and go for it! Taste the sweetness of the project and make it your way. There is no wrong or right way to creativity. In the long run there is only YOUR WAY!

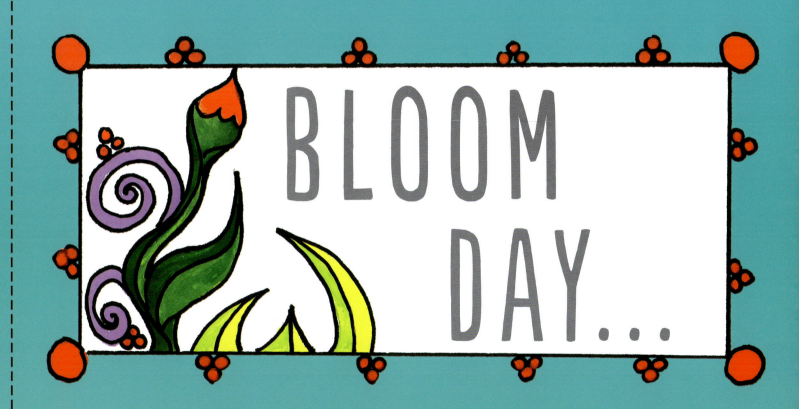

Use your energy today for rebirth and growth. Celebrate your own bloom. Stretch your roots…**renew yourself.**

"…and the day came when the risk it took to remain tight in the bud was more painful than the risk it took to blossom." –Anais Nin

What a wonderful quote, and this is what the permission slip is about. Use your energies to grow today. The risk is small compared to the reward you will receive from yourself. It is amazing how we really are our own gardeners. Sometimes we just need to pull a few weeds, apply a little love, and gently care for ourselves in order to plant our roots down and begin our growth. Begin the process, prepare your soil, stretch and begin to burst from your bud and bloom!

Listen closely to your inner voice. You know that "gut" reaction? It's your own personal sign post. Pay attention to what YOU have to say to YOU.

Has your inner voice been whispering to you? Is it telling you to go ahead and do those things NOW? Is it wondering "WHAT" it is that you are waiting for? This permission slip allows you to listen to your inner voice as opposed to your inner critic. Hear what it is that you are positively saying to yourself, take that gut advice, and put it into action, because time waits for no man (or woman). Listen closely.

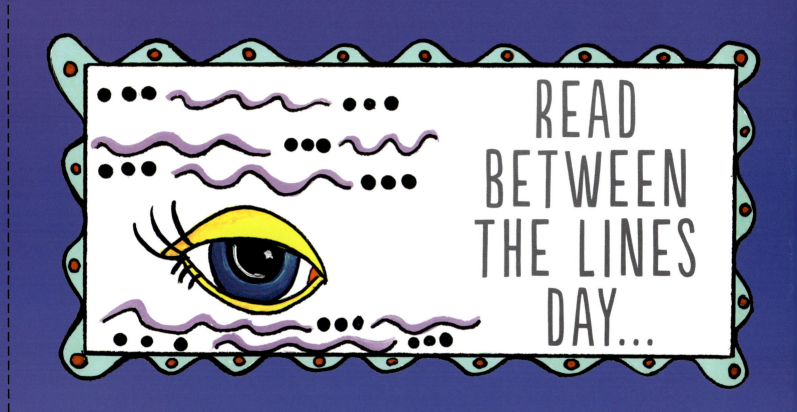

Pay attention. Ask yourself questions today and read between the lines. Recognize the difference between your verbal and your nonverbal messages.

WOW! Usually everyone tells you NOT to do this, but today GO FOR IT! Ask yourself some small questions today. Am I happy? The way to read between the lines is to see if you are smiling from the inside out. Pay attention to what you are saying out loud and what you are saying in your head, and in your body. When we do not honor our true feelings and thoughts, we cannot continue forward in a positive way. Read between the lines of what others want the answer to be and what you know the answer to be.

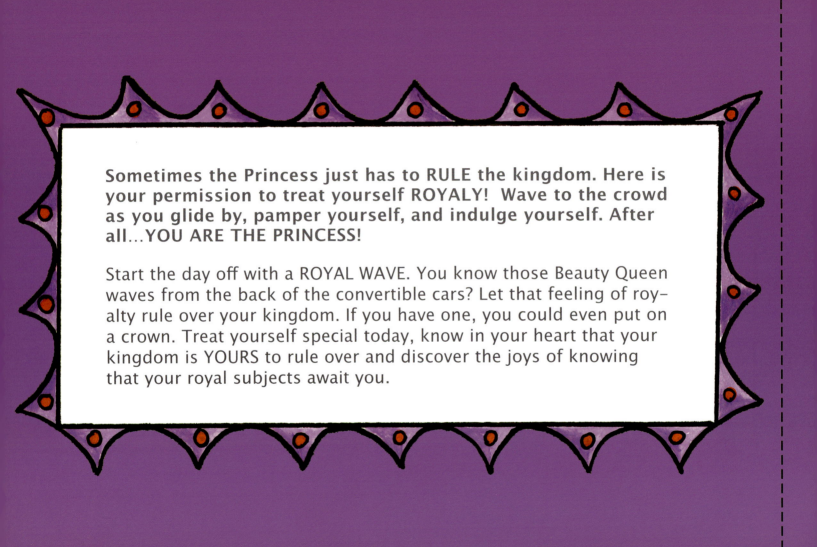

Sometimes the Princess just has to RULE the kingdom. Here is your permission to treat yourself ROYALY! Wave to the crowd as you glide by, pamper yourself, and indulge yourself. After all...YOU ARE THE PRINCESS!

Start the day off with a ROYAL WAVE. You know those Beauty Queen waves from the back of the convertible cars? Let that feeling of royalty rule over your kingdom. If you have one, you could even put on a crown. Treat yourself special today, know in your heart that your kingdom is YOURS to rule over and discover the joys of knowing that your royal subjects await you.

Take a moment...BREATHE. Listen closely to what your heart is telling you and then take another deep breath.

There are so many of us who can use this card on any given day. Sometimes we hear what our heart is saying, but we dismiss it too quickly. Other times we ignore it completely, or perhaps don't even hear it. All of your answers are there within you if you just take the time to listen. Once you hear the message, let it become a part of you mentally and then follow your direction, feel your wings starting to bud, and begin to stretch them like a baby bird. Or, if you are ready, walk to the edge and JUMP. Those wings from your heart will glide you on your way.

Look for new possibilities. Broaden your horizons. You determine your path. Set your intentions and turn the handle.

Are there so many things that you want to do? Are there doors to be opened that you know all you have to do is turn the handle and enter in? This permission slip allows you to turn the handle and give all your dreams a POSITIVE greeting. If you do not open the door, you will never know and will stand outside your dreams with that woulda, shoulda, coulda. THAT JUST WON'T DO! Go ahead... don't even bother to ring the door bell. Just turn the handle to the doors of your dreams and say HELLO!

Go ahead... toot your own horn today. Remind yourself of the specialness that makes you... YOU! Rejoice in all that you are and all that you do.

Free yourself today. Tell your story. You can do this in so many different ways: journal, paint, take a picture, take pride in your job or family. By telling your story, you break down barriers. You allow yourself to realize the unique footprint that is YOU! So go ahead... start up the band and toot that horn. Then sit back and ENJOY THE MUSIC.

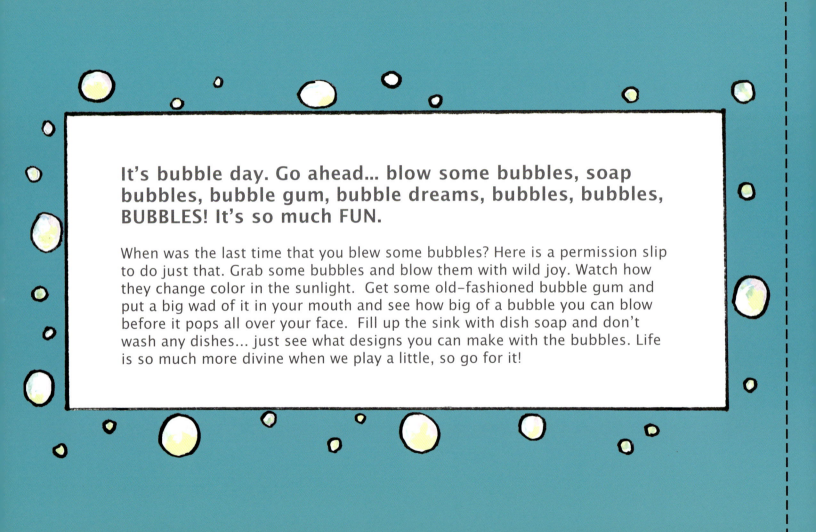

It's bubble day. Go ahead... blow some bubbles, soap bubbles, bubble gum, bubble dreams, bubbles, bubbles, BUBBLES! It's so much FUN.

When was the last time that you blew some bubbles? Here is a permission slip to do just that. Grab some bubbles and blow them with wild joy. Watch how they change color in the sunlight. Get some old-fashioned bubble gum and put a big wad of it in your mouth and see how big of a bubble you can blow before it pops all over your face. Fill up the sink with dish soap and don't wash any dishes... just see what designs you can make with the bubbles. Life is so much more divine when we play a little, so go for it!

Find the humor in things today. It will do you GOOD! See things with the FUNNY SIDE UP! People will catch on and everyone will be laughing.

Ok, so you are up to your elbows in work, tension in your neck and you're frustrated. You could throw in the towel, have a good cry or you could find the humor in things. You could give a good wiggle in your chair to keep your hands and feet active. You could sing a song while doing the laundry. You could ride on the ledge of the shopping cart like a kid. Sometimes it is just with a smile that we start to find happiness, SO SMILE! Then let that smile turn into a LAUGH and then, well... before you know it, you'll be laughing all day.

Go ahead…plump up your pillow, grab your favorite blanket and take a nap. What are you waiting for?

Are you having one of those days where you have good intentions of doing A LOT of work, but your energy levels are so low that you are seeing double? Do you have a moment, a secret spot to go to where you can TAKE A NAP? Sometimes you just have to do that. Naps are wonderful things that we give to ourselves to replenish, to energize and just allow our brains to slow down. Here is a permission slip. Use it whenever you like. SWEET DREAMS!

Today, remember to be more nurturing to others, knowing that all your words and actions have an impact on those around you. So, pay it forward. It FEELS so GOOD!

There is an old saying that goes "the more you give, the more you receive." In this fast-paced world of ours, take a moment out and think of how you can give to someone else, like a pat on the back for a job well done, or taking a moment to say HI to the person next to you in line. You can also volunteer at the local boys and girls club, a local hospital or anywhere your positive spirit can be used. This is such a simple thing to do, and YES, you do have time. Once you start to pay it forward, you'll wonder why you didn't do it before.

Go ahead…put them on. It's Rose-Colored Glasses Day! See everything from a "pink" side with no shades of blue. If someone says Black, say Pink. Everyone will wonder what has gotten into you. Just give the reply…everything is just ROSEY!

Is the weather grey and gloomy today? Wanting to bury yourself under the covers and wait for a better day? I think we all know that feeling. So, today is Rose-Colored Glasses day. I know that someone probably told you NOT to look at the world through them, but this permission slip says to go for it. Sometimes, if we just see the same situation in a different light, it can change our whole vision on things. It just might turn you around!

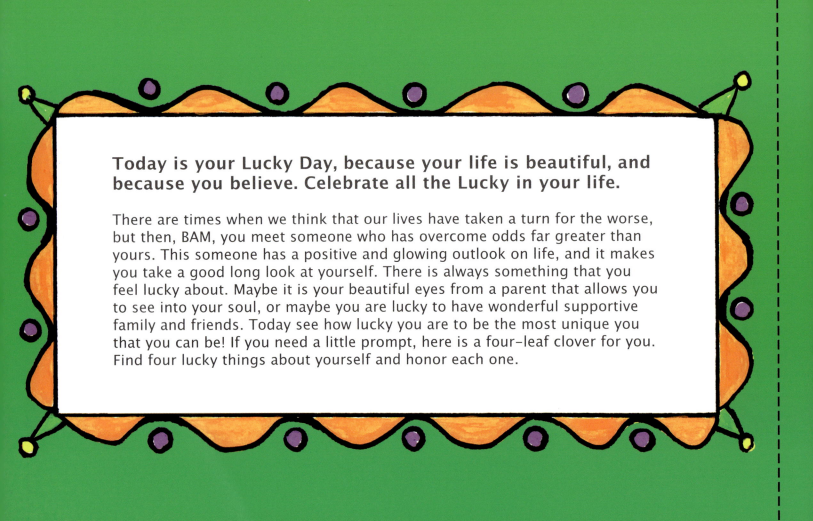

Today is your Lucky Day, because your life is beautiful, and because you believe. Celebrate all the Lucky in your life.

There are times when we think that our lives have taken a turn for the worse, but then, BAM, you meet someone who has overcome odds far greater than yours. This someone has a positive and glowing outlook on life, and it makes you take a good long look at yourself. There is always something that you feel lucky about. Maybe it is your beautiful eyes from a parent that allows you to see into your soul, or maybe you are lucky to have wonderful supportive family and friends. Today see how lucky you are to be the most unique you that you can be! If you need a little prompt, here is a four-leaf clover for you. Find four lucky things about yourself and honor each one.

Find the comfortable seat today, find a moment to breathe and find your comfort zone.

There are many times in life that we think that throwing in the towel is the only answer. But if we just take a moment to sit down, to breathe deeply, we can usually find the comfort again. When we take the opportunity to see the smallest of wonders to bring us happiness, when we open up our heart to change and embrace the lesson that it has to provide us, we renew our soul. Life can become comfortable anytime we take a moment to see all the beauty around us.

"LET IT GO"! Let go of the parts of the past that serve you no purpose. Let go of the people who drain your energy. It will feel like a big rock has been lifted off you.

This is not an easy permission slip, but it is one that most of us need to have in our back pocket, our wallet, or even posted on the fridge. We tend to hold on to things that serve us no purpose, or quite simply drain our energy. So why is that? Sometimes it is best to cut your strings, even if it is something that you hold on to because of age, because of fear, or because of sentiment. You will feel better, breathe easier, and believe in yourself more. Give it a try. Let it go.

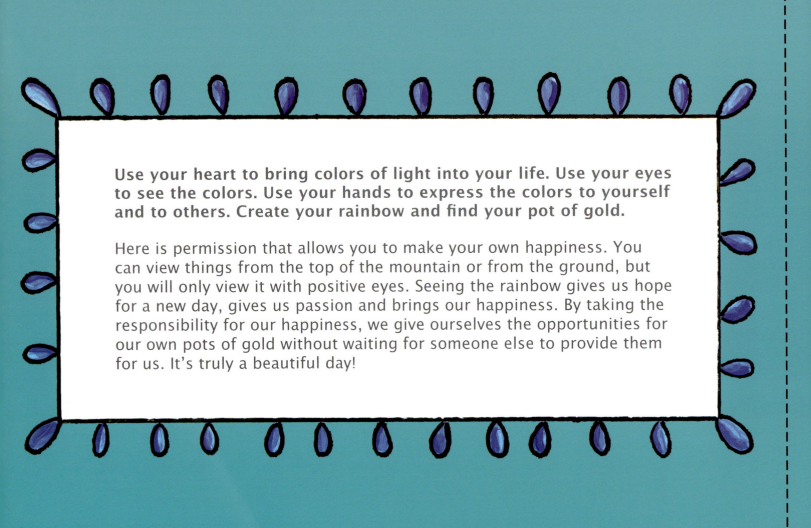

Use your heart to bring colors of light into your life. Use your eyes to see the colors. Use your hands to express the colors to yourself and to others. Create your rainbow and find your pot of gold.

Here is permission that allows you to make your own happiness. You can view things from the top of the mountain or from the ground, but you will only view it with positive eyes. Seeing the rainbow gives us hope for a new day, gives us passion and brings our happiness. By taking the responsibility for our happiness, we give ourselves the opportunities for our own pots of gold without waiting for someone else to provide them for us. It's truly a beautiful day!

Here is your permission to "OPEN UP" yourself to love, to do something new, to take a risk, to dance, to sing or choose to do more. OPEN UP and see what is before you and within you!

When we start to venture into areas that we are NOT completely familiar with, sometimes we are really excited and just jump right in. Other times we pull back and start to make excuses for why we CAN'T venture in. Break that excuse right down and allow yourself to venture in and bypass all the negativity. Find permission whenever you feel yourself slipping backwards, or whenever you need that little nudge forward. Take a risk at something you are dreaming of and OPEN UP! You just might find something new to love about yourself.

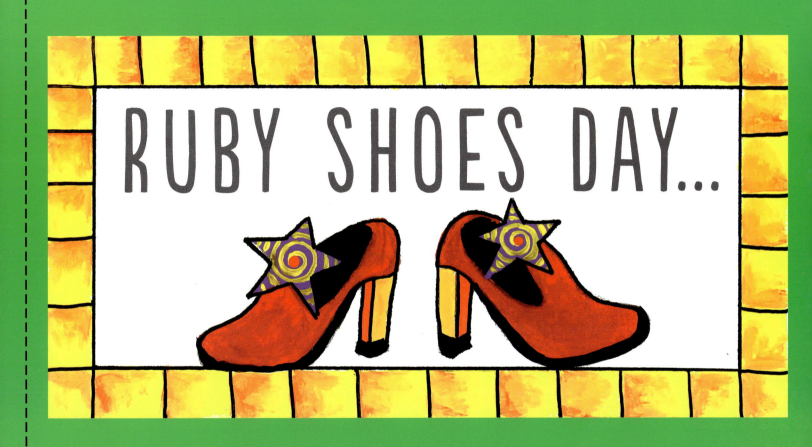

"You had the power all along, my dear." –Glinda, the Good Witch.

Put on your ruby shoes and walk in your own power, dance, sing and create. Walk away from any fear that you have.

Did you ever have one of those days where you just questioned why you do what you do? Or better yet, why you aren't doing what you want to do? This permission slip can help make your dreams come true, and all you have to do is click your heels, and you are exactly where you want to be. Recognize your own power. By doing so, you will realize that the fear is much weaker when we BELIEVE in ourselves. So, go ahead, click those heels three times!

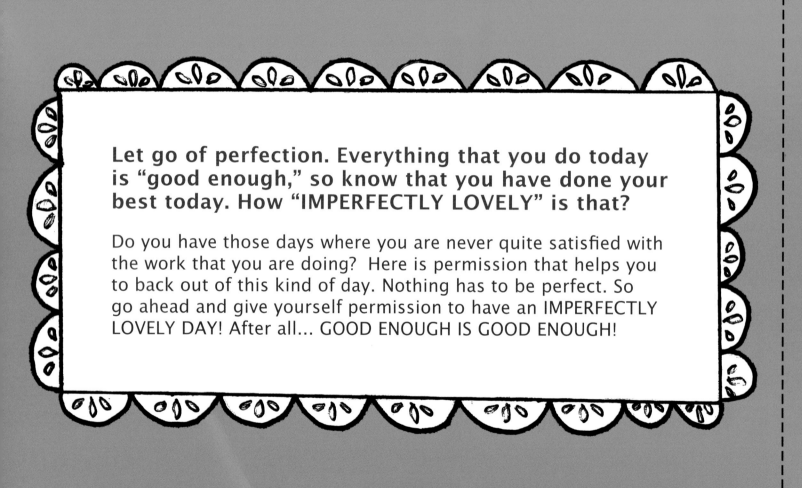

Let go of perfection. Everything that you do today is "good enough," so know that you have done your best today. How "IMPERFECTLY LOVELY" is that?

Do you have those days where you are never quite satisfied with the work that you are doing? Here is permission that helps you to back out of this kind of day. Nothing has to be perfect. So go ahead and give yourself permission to have an IMPERFECTLY LOVELY DAY! After all... GOOD ENOUGH IS GOOD ENOUGH!

Light a candle or go outside when the first stars appear and make a wish for yourself. Place your heart in your hands and wish for the highest star to fly upon.

It doesn't have to be your birthday for you to make a wish for yourself. We can hold the highest wishes anytime, any day, and in any moment. Making wishes for yourself to honor anything helps you to acknowledge who you are and where you wish to go. So go ahead... here is permission to do just that. Make a wish for yourself. It could be the same one every day or it could be a different one, and then BELIEVE in the wish, so that it may come true. WISHES DO COME TRUE!

Celebrate your time today, taking time to honor who you are and what you do. Honor your path, your love, and your creativity. HAVE FUN!

As women, we are always the first to give our time and our energy to everyone. We are the caregivers, the daughters, the mothers, and the wives. This permission card is just for us. The gift to do whatever it is that you desire. It might be something creative, or it might be taking a long hot bath and lighting a special candle that you bought just because it was sweet smelling and made you happy. No matter what it is, enjoy who you are and all that you do for everyone else. It's a beautiful thing.

Do not hurry forward, but rather be right here in the present and enjoy every moment of it. After all... right now is what matters the most. ENJOY YOUR PRESENT!

We all do it: the "I have to get to," the "I must finish," and the "tomorrow I am going to." We project ourselves into the future without really being aware of it. Here is permission that allows you to stay in the present and become suddenly aware of the wondrous life you are having right now. After all... it's this day that matters because we'll never have it back again. Enjoy today, laugh a little longer, smile a little wider and love a little deeper.